D.I.Y. Doughnuts: 60 #Delish Homemade Doughnut Recipes

RHONDA BELLE

Copyright © 2016 Rhonda Belle
All rights reserved.

ISBN-13: 978-1539891864

ISBN-10: 1539891860

DEDICATION

To Foodies Everywhere...Enjoy & Be Well!

Table of Contents
Delight in Homemade Doughnuts... 8

- Amazing Apple Cider Doughnuts 9
- Apple Cream Doughnut Drops 9
- Apple Juice Doughnuts 10
- Baked Cinnamon Swirl Doughnuts 10
- Banana Sweet Hearts 11
- Blackberry Doughnuts 11
- Blueberry Butterflies 12
- Buttermilk Jelly Doughnuts 12
- Cheery Cherry Drops 13
- Chocolate Raised Doughnuts (Diabetic) 13
- Cinnamon Twists 14
- Coconut Cake Doughnuts 14
- Crazy Creams 15
- Crullers 15
- Delicious Date Doughnuts 16
- Double Chocolate Doughnuts 16
- Doughnut Popovers 17
- Ginger Nuts 17
- Gingerbread Doughnuts 18
- Golden Puffs 18
- Holiday Eggnog Doughnuts 19
- Honey-Maple Glazed Doughnuts 19
- Huckleberry Fritters 20
- Italian Style Doughnuts 20
- Juicy Jelly Doughnuts 21
- Lemon Coconut Balls 22
- Lemon Cream Cake Doughnuts 22
- Lingonberry Doughnuts 23
- Mashed Potato Doughnuts 23
- Mini-Maple Nuts 24
- Mouthwatering Molasses Doughnuts 24
- New Orleans Style Doughnuts 25
- Nutmeg Doughnuts 25
- October Spice Doughnuts 26
- Old Fashioned Cake Doughnuts 26

Orange Glazed Doughnuts 27
Oven-Baked Sour Cream Doughnuts 27
Potluck Cake Doughnuts 28
Powdered Doughnuts I 28
Powdered Sugar Doughnuts II 29
Pretty Peach Fritters 29
Pumpkin Doughnuts 29
Purely Pineapple Doughnuts 30
Raspberry Jam Doughnuts 30
Sour Cream & Banana Doughnuts 31
Sourdough Applesauce Doughnuts 31
Southern Sweet Milk Doughnuts 32
Spiced Maple Doughnuts 32
Strawberry Fields Doughnuts 33
Sugar Cane Doughnuts 33
Sugar N' Spice Doughnuts 33
Summer Squash Doughnuts 34
Sunday Dinner Doughnuts 34
Sweet Treat Doughnut Holes 35
Sweet Cream Doughnuts 35
Traditional Raised Doughnuts 35
Very Vanilla Doughnuts 36
White Chocolate Cake Doughnuts 36
World's Easiest Doughnuts 37
Yummy Buttermilk Doughnuts 37

ACKNOWLEDGEMENTS

To the love of my life, Johnny.
You are Mommy's greatest inspiration.

To my Mom & Dad (Sunset February 2016).
Love you always...

Delight in Homemade Doughnuts...

Nothing is better than a batch of fresh doughnuts made from scratch in your very own kitchen. These wonderful recipes will help you create delicious doughnuts, doughnut holes, fritters, crullers and more. For delectable treats that promise to bring pure joy, try these helpful tips:

- Using yeast is common when making fresh dough. The length of time it will take for a yeast dough to rise depends in part on the surrounding room temperature. Don't try to speed things along by allowing your dough to get too warm. Excess heat can kill the yeast and even prematurely cook a portion of the dough.
- Less flour makes a softer dough and light, tender doughnuts. More flour creates a cake-like texture (which is also awesome).
- You'll know that the dough is ready if an indention remains after poking your dough with a finger.
- Steel doughnut cutters offer an even size cut each time. 3"-4" sizes are common and can be purchased at big box retail stores that sell kitchen utensils. You can also improvise with a biscuit cutter. In either case, flour your cutting tool before each cut to prevent sticking.
- Canola oil is a great choice for frying, but peanut oil has a higher smoking point and is also a good choice. Otherwise, for amazing taste go with Crisco or solid shortening, if the recipe allows. Aim for a minimum 1-2" oil depth for frying.
- High sides are best for doughnut making. Deep fryers, Dutch ovens and stockpots work well. *Keep the kiddies out of the kitchen for safety.*
- 375°F is common for oil temps. You can check using a thermometer or a day old cube of bread. If the bread browns within 60 seconds, you can be assured the oil is ready.
- Slide doughnuts gently into oil to prevent splatter. Dropping doughnut batter into hot fat eliminates the need for rolling and cutting, but be sure to do so carefully and close to the oil. Avoid dropping from on high and take care not to burn yourself (or others).
- Fry only as many doughnuts at one time as can float easily in oil or shortening. Overcrowding will not produce good results.
- When turning or lifting doughnuts, take extra care not to pierce them. This will allow additional oil to seep in and ruin your finished treat.
- For draining excess oil or glazing, cover a large portion of countertop with wax paper or paper towels and top with a wire cooling rack.

Amazing Apple Cider Doughnuts

¼ cup solid vegetable shortening
¼ teaspoon nutmeg
½ cup buttermilk
½ teaspoon cinnamon
½ teaspoon salt
1 cup apple cider
1 cup granulated sugar
1 teaspoon baking soda
2 large eggs
2 teaspoons baking powder
3½ cups all-purpose flour
Vegetable oil or shortening (for frying)
APPLE GLAZE:
¼ cup apple cider
2 cups confectioners' sugar

Boil apple cider in small saucepan until it is reduced to ¼ cup, 8 to 10 minutes; cool. Beat sugar with shortening until smooth. Add eggs and mix well, then add buttermilk and reduced cider. Stir together flour, baking powder, baking soda, cinnamon, salt and nutmeg in another bowl. Add to liquid ingredients; mix just enough to combine. Transfer dough to lightly floured board and pat to ½" thickness. Cut with a 2½ to 3 inch doughnut cutter. *You can reserve doughnut holes and re-roll and cut scraps.* Add enough oil or shortening to fill a deep pan 3 inches; heat to 375 degrees. Fry several doughnuts at a time, turning once or twice, until browned and cooked through, about 4 minutes. Remove to paper towels with slotted spoon. *For glaze*: mix confectioners' sugar and cider. Dip doughnuts while warm; serve warm. #Delish!

Apple Cream Doughnut Drops

½ teaspoon nutmeg
1 cup whipped cream
1 teaspoon cinnamon
1 teaspoon salt
1½ cups grated raw apples
1¾ cup buttermilk
2 cups sugar
2 teaspoons baking soda
5 eggs, beaten
7 cups flour
Vegetable oil or shortening (for frying)

Beat eggs, add sugar and beat well. Add remaining ingredients. Drop by teaspoon into about 3 inches of oil heated to about 400 degrees. Fry until golden brown. Check to see that they are cooked all the way through. Drain on a paper towel. Serve plain or roll in sugar. Makes over 100 balls. #Delish!

Apple Juice Doughnuts
¼ cup sugar
½ cup half-and-half
½ teaspoon cinnamon
½ teaspoon cinnamon
½ teaspoon nutmeg
½ teaspoon salt
1 egg, slightly beaten
1/3 cup frozen apple juice concentrate, thawed
1/3 cup sugar
2 cups flour
3 teaspoons baking powder
Vegetable oil or shortening (for frying)

In a deep fryer or heavy 3-quart saucepan, heat 3" to 4" oil to 375 degrees. Lightly spoon flour into measuring cup; level off. In a large bowl, combine flour, ¼ cup sugar, baking powder, salt, ½ teaspoon cinnamon and nutmeg; blend well. Add half-and-half, apple juice concentrate and egg; stir with fork until thoroughly mixed. Drop by the teaspoonful into hot oil, 5 or 6 at a time. Fry doughnut balls 1 to 1½ minutes on each side or until golden brown. Drain on paper towels. In small bowl or plastic bag, combine 1/3 cup sugar and ½ teaspoon cinnamon; roll warm doughnuts in mixture. Makes about 30 to 35 doughnut balls. #Delish!

Baked Cinnamon Swirl Doughnuts
½ cup butter or margarine
½ teaspoon cinnamon
½ teaspoon nutmeg, ground
1 teaspoon lemon peel, grated
1 teaspoon salt
2 cups milk, divided
2 cups powdered sugar, sifted
2 eggs
2 packages active dry yeast
2/3 cup sugar
5 cups flour, divided

Combine 2 cups flour, sugar, yeast, salt, lemon peel and nutmeg in a large bowl. Combine 1¾ cups milk and butter in 1 quart saucepan. Heat over low heat just until butter begins to melt. Gradually beat milk mix into the flour mix with electric mixer at low speed. Increase speed to medium; beat 2 minutes scraping down side of bowl once. Beat in eggs and 1 cup flour at low speed. Increase speed to medium; beat 2 minutes, scraping down side of bowl once. Stir in enough additional flour, about 2 cups with wooden spoon to make soft dough. Cover with greased plastic wrap; refrigerate for a minimum of 2 hours up to 24 hours. Punch down dough. Turn out dough onto lightly floured surface. Knead about 1 minute or until the dough is no longer sticky, adding remaining ½ cup flour to prevent sticking if necessary. Next, grease 2 large baking sheets. Roll out dough to ½" thickness with lightly floured rolling pin. Cut dough with floured 2¾" doughnut cutter. Reroll scraps, reserving doughnut holes. Place doughnuts and holes 2" apart on prepared baking sheets. Cover with towels; let rise in a warm place for a half hour or until doubled in bulk. *To prepare glaze:* Combine powdered sugar and cinnamon in small bowl. Stir in enough remaining milk, about ¼ cup to thin glaze to desired consistency. Cover and set aside. Preheat oven to 400 degrees. Place pieces of waxed paper under wire racks to keep counter clean. Bake doughnuts and holes 8-10 minutes or until golden brown. Remove from pan with spatula; cool on wire racks 5 minutes. Dip warm doughnuts into glaze. Place right side up on racks, allowing glaze to drip down sides. Serve warm and enjoy!

Banana Sweet Hearts

¼ cup margarine
½ teaspoon ground cinnamon
½ teaspoon ground nutmeg
¾ cup sugar
1 cup bananas, mashed
1 teaspoon salt
2 large eggs, beaten
3 cups peanut oil, for frying
4 cups all-purpose flour
4 teaspoons baking powder
TOPPING:
¾ cup sugar
2 teaspoons ground cinnamon

Heat oil in a deep-fat fryer or deep heavy skillet. In a large bowl, combine flour, sugar, baking powder, salt, cinnamon, and nutmeg. Cut in margarine and mix well. Make a well in the center of the mix and add mashed bananas and eggs. Mix well with a wooden spoon or your hands. Place dough on a lightly floured surface and roll to ½" thick. Cut with a 2½" doughnut cutter that you dip in flour as needed. Deep fry, a few at a time, until golden brown. Drain on brown paper bags. Fry the doughnut "holes" also. Combine sugar and cinnamon in a paper bag or place on a shallow plate. Coat warm doughnuts with this mixture. Makes about 22 doughnuts and 22 holes. #Delish!

Blackberry Doughnuts

¾ cup sugar
¾ teaspoon cinnamon
1 can (10 ounces) refrigerated buttermilk biscuits (fluffy variety)
1/3 cup blackberry jelly
6 tablespoons butter or margarine, melted

Heat oven to 375 degrees. Place melted margarine in small bowl; set aside. In another small bowl, combine sugar and cinnamon; set aside. Stir jelly until smooth. Seal tip of a large baster with foil. Remove rubber bulb. Spoon jelly into baster; replace bulb. Bake biscuits as directed on can. Immediately dip each hot biscuit in melted margarine, coating all sides. Roll in sugar mixture, heavily coating all sides of each biscuit. Insert baster in side of each biscuit; squeeze small amount of jelly into center. (Refill baster as needed.) Serve warm or cold. #Delish!

Blueberry Butterflies
¼ cup milk
½ teaspoon baking soda
1 cup buttermilk
1 cup sugar
1 pinch salt
1 pint fresh blueberries, rinsed, hulled, and patted dry
1 teaspoon baking powder
2 cups powdered sugar
2 eggs
2 tablespoons solid vegetable shortening
3½ cups all-purpose flour

Using a standing mixer fitted with a paddle attachment, cream the shortening and sugar. Add the eggs, one at a time and beat until incorporated. With the machine running, slowly add the buttermilk. Switch the paddle attachment to a dough hook and add the blueberries. Sift together the flour, salt, baking powder and baking soda. Add the flour mixture, 1 cup at a time, until the dough forms a smooth ball and climbs up the dough hook. Place the dough in a greased bowl, turning once and cover with plastic wrap. Refrigerate for 1 hour. Preheat a deep fryer to 350 degrees. Turn the dough out onto a floured surface and roll out to ½" thick. Using a doughnut cutter, cut the dough into rounds. Fry the doughnuts in batches until golden brown. Remove and drain on paper towels. In small bowl, whisk together the milk and powdered sugar. Drizzle the glaze over each doughnut and allow to sit until the glaze sets. Serve the doughnuts on a platter. Makes 24 doughnuts. #Delish!

Buttermilk Jelly Doughnuts
¼ teaspoon baking soda
½ cup buttermilk
½ cup sugar
½ teaspoon salt
½ teaspoon vanilla extract
1 cup or so thick jam or preserves of your choice
1 teaspoon baking powder
1½ cups plus 2 tablespoons all-purpose flour
2 large eggs
2 tablespoons unsalted butter, melted
Vegetable oil or shortening (for frying)
SUGAR COATING:
½ cup powdered sugar
½ cup sugar

Combine all dry ingredients in a large bowl, stirring well to combine thoroughly. Whisk together buttermilk, eggs and vanilla, mixing well. Blend the liquid mixture with the melted butter and add to the dry ingredients, mixing with a wooden spoon until the dough is formed. The dough will be very sticky which is necessary to yield light doughnuts. Refrigerate dough for 30 minutes to make it easier to handle. Sprinkle the 2 additional tablespoons of flour over a clean, dry work surface and gently coax the dough into a ball. *Do not add flour...it will create a tough dough which is not desirable for this recipe.* Turn soft dough out onto floured work surface. Gently press the dough into a 9" x 7" rectangle, about 1/3 to ½" thick. Cut dough into rounds of your chosen size with a cookie cutter. Place a teaspoon or so of thick jam in the middle of one dough round then cover with another round of dough, creating a sandwich. Press seams together firmly to seal. Pour approximately 8 cups of oil in a deep heavy bottomed pot to 365 degrees. Fry the doughnuts in small batches for about 1 minute or so on each side or until golden brown. Makes about 1 dozen. #Delish!

Cheery Cherry Drops
½ cup milk
½ tablespoon cinnamon
1 teaspoon vanilla
2 egg whites
2 egg yolks
2 ounces sugar
2 tablespoons cherry brandy
2 teaspoons baking powder
3 ounces butter
9 ounces flour
9 ounces sour cherries
Vegetable oil or shortening (for frying)
Cream butter, sugar, vanilla, cinnamon and egg yolks until creamy. Next, mix baking powder under flour and mix, alternating with the milk and the brandy under the butter mix. Beat the egg whites until stiff and fold into dough mix. Add the drained cherries or apple slices to the entire mix. Heat about 3" of oil in deep fryer and put tablespoons full of the dough into oil heated to about 350 degrees, and bake until doughnuts are golden brown. Drain on paper towels. Serve warm. #Delish!

Chocolate Raised Doughnuts (Diabetic)
¼ cup solid shortening
¼ cup warm water
½ cup skim milk
½ teaspoon salt
1 egg
1 packet dry yeast
1/3 cup unsweetened baking cocoa
1/8 teaspoon Stevia
2 tablespoons granulated fructose
2½ cups all-purpose flour
Rebaudiana extract
Pour skim milk into a small saucepan, bring to a boil, remove from the heat and allow to cool. Dissolve the yeast in the warm water. Combine skim milk, yeast mixture, sweetener of your choice, shortening, fructose, egg and salt in a large mixing bowl. Combine the cocoa with 1¼ cups of flour in another bowl. Stir to mix. Add to liquid mixture in bowl. Beat on low until mixture is blended and smooth. Add remaining flour and stir until all the flour is incorporated into the dough. Turn out onto a lightly floured surface; then knead for 4 to 5 minutes or until dough is smooth and elastic. Place in a greased bowl, turn dough over, cover, and allow to rise until double in size (about 1½ hours). Punch dough down and roll to about ½" thickness. Cut with floured

doughnut cutter. Place doughnuts onto a greased cookie sheet or piece of waxed paper. Cover and allow to rise. Heat 2" to 3" of oil in deep fat fryer or heavy saucepan to 375 degrees. Heat using a wide spatula in the oil. Gently slide spatula under a doughnut. Place doughnut in the hot oil and fry about 2 minutes on each side. Remove from oil; drain on paper towels. Repeat with remaining doughnuts. Makes about 18 total. #Delish!

Cinnamon Twists

¼ cup butter or margarine, softened
¼ cup sugar
½ cup warm milk
¾ cup warm water, divided
1 egg
1 package (¼ ounces) active dry yeast
1½ teaspoons salt
4 to 4½ cups all-purpose flour
CINNAMON FILLING:
¼ cup butter or margarine, melted
½ cup packed brown sugar
4 teaspoons ground cinnamon

In a large mixing bowl, dissolve yeast in ¼ cup warm water. Add 2 cups of flour, sugar, salt, milk, butter, egg and remaining water; beat on medium speed for 2 minutes. Stir in enough remaining flour to form a soft dough. Turn onto a floured board; knead until smooth and elastic, about 6-8 minutes. Place in a greased bowl, turning once to grease top. Cover and let rise in a warm place until doubled, about 1 hour. Punch down. Roll into a 16" x 12" rectangle. Brush with butter. Combine brown sugar and cinnamon; sprinkle over butter. Let dough rest for 6 minutes. Cut lengthwise into three 16" x 4" strips. Cut each strip into sixteen 4" x 1" pieces. Twist and place on greased baking sheets. Cover and let rise until doubled, about 30 minutes. Bake at 350 degrees for 15 minutes or until golden. Remove and let cool a bit. Serve and enjoy!

Coconut Cake Doughnuts

¼ cup milk
½ cup flaked coconut
½ cup granulated sugar
½ teaspoon salt
2 eggs
2 tablespoons melted shortening or vegetable oil
2-1/3 cups sifted all-purpose flour

Beat eggs with sugar until light; add milk and cook shortening. Add sifted dry ingredients and coconut; stir just until blended. Chill several hours. Roll out onto a lightly floured surface to ½" thickness. Cut out doughnuts with a doughnut cutter. Fry in deep, hot oil (about 375 degrees) until brown; turn and brown other side (about 1 minute per side). Drain on paper towels. Sprinkle with confectioners' sugar and additional coconut if desired. Makes 1 dozen. #Delish!

Crazy Creams

¼ cup warm water
½ cup white sugar
1½ cups lukewarm milk
1½ teaspoon vanilla
1 quart vegetable oil for frying
1 teaspoon salt
1/3 cup butter
1/3 cup shortening
2 (.25 ounce) envelopes active dry yeast
2 cups confectioners' sugar
2 eggs
4 tablespoons hot water or as needed
5 cups all-purpose flour

Sprinkle the yeast over the warm water, and let stand for 5 minutes, or until foamy. In a large bowl, mix together the yeast mixture, milk, sugar, salt, eggs, shortening, and 2 cups of the flour. Mix for a few minutes at low speed, or stirring with a wooden spoon. Beat in remaining flour ½ cup at a time, until the dough no longer sticks to the bowl. Knead for about 5 minutes, or until smooth and elastic. Place the dough into a greased bowl and cover. Set in a warm place to rise until dough doubles in size. Turn the dough out onto a floured surface, and gently roll out to ½" thickness. Cut with a floured doughnut cutter. Let doughnuts sit out to rise again until double. Cover loosely with a cloth. Next, heat oil in a deep fryer or a large heavy skillet to about 350 degrees. Slide doughnuts into the hot oil using a wide spatula. Turn over as they rise to the surface. Fry doughnuts on each side until golden brown. Remove from hot oil and drain. *For glaze*: Melt butter in a saucepan over medium heat. Stir in confectioners' sugar and vanilla until smooth. Remove from heat, and stir in hot water one tablespoon at a time until the icing is somewhat thin, but not too watery. Dip doughnuts into the glaze while still hot and set onto wire racks with paper towels underneath to drain. #Delish!

Crullers

¼ cup milk
¼ cup shortening
¼ teaspoon mace, nutmeg or vanilla
½ teaspoon salt
¾ cup sugar
2 eggs, separated
3 teaspoons baking powder
3½ cups flour (or a little more)
Vegetable oil or shortening (for frying)

Cream shortening and sugar together until light; add the well beaten yolks of eggs. Sift the flour, baking powder, salt and spice and add alternately with the milk, then fold in the stiffly beaten egg whites, and then enough flour to make dough stiff. Place on a floured board, roll to ¾" inch thick and cut with cruller cutter, or a small glass and thimble for center. Fry in hot oil. Remove from fat with wire spoon or fork, drain on paper towel. Sprinkle with cinnamon or powdered sugar. #Delish!

Delicious Date Doughnuts

¼ teaspoon ground nutmeg
½ teaspoon salt
¾ cup granulated sugar
1 cup dates, chopped
1 cup milk
1 tablespoon melted butter
1 teaspoon lemon extract
2 eggs, beaten
2½ cups all-purpose flour
2½ teaspoons baking powder
Vegetable oil or shortening (for frying)

In a bowl, combine beaten eggs, sugar and melted butter; beat well. In another bowl, combine flour with baking powder, salt and nutmeg. Fold in dates. Add dry ingredients to egg mixture alternately with milk and lemon extract. Heat oil in deep fryer to 375 degrees. Drop batter by the tablespoonful, 2 or 3 at a time, into hot oil and fry until brown, about 3 minutes, turning once. Drain on paper towels. Make 3 to 4 dozen doughnuts. #Delish!

Double Chocolate Doughnuts

¼ cup cocoa powder
¼ cup hot water
¼ cup powdered sugar
¼ cup sugar
½ cup cake flour
½ ounce dry yeast (Two ¼ ounce packages)
½ teaspoon salt
¾ cup all-purpose flour
¾ teaspoon baking soda
1/3 cup warm water
3 ounces semisweet chocolate, melted
6 ounces baking potato, like russets, cooked, peeled and riced
Canola oil, for frying
<u>CHOCOLATE GLAZE:</u>
½ cup cream
4 ounces semisweet chocolate, chopped

In a bowl, combine yeast, warm water and sugar to dissolve. Add ¼ cup of the all-purpose flour and ¼ cup of the cake flour. Stir and set in a warm place for 30 minutes. The yeast will foam. Next, combine cocoa powder, baking soda and hot water to dissolve. Add the melted chocolate to the cocoa powder mixture, then stir in the powdered sugar, salt and potato. Add this to the foamed yeast along with another ¼ cup of all-purpose flour and the remaining ¼ cup of cake flour and mix on low to combine with a paddle. Mix on high speed for 30 seconds to combine. Add the remaining ¼ cup of all-purpose flour and mix on high speed. Next, flour the work surface heavily and knead the dough gently until sticky and well-blended. Turn into a greased bowl and proof until doubled in bulk, about 1½ hours. Turn dough out onto a floured surface and punch down then proof for another 30 minutes. Flour work surface heavily and pat out dough to about ½" thick. Cut out doughnuts and holes with a cutter, flouring the cutter each time to prevent sticking, and set on a floured sheet pan. Heat oil to 375 degrees and drop in doughnuts and holes. Cook doughnuts for 45 to 60 seconds and the holes for 30 seconds, flipping once. Drain on a paper towel-lined sheet pan. *To make glaze*: Place the chopped chocolate in a bowl. Boil the cream and pour it over the chocolate and let sit, whisking to combine. Keep warm. Dip freshly cooked doughnuts in chocolate glaze when cooled. #Delish!

Doughnut Popovers
¼ teaspoon cinnamon
¼ teaspoon salt
1 cup granulated sugar
1 cup sweet milk
1 teaspoon vanilla
2 eggs, beaten
2 tablespoons butter, melted
3 cups flour
3 teaspoon nutmeg
Vegetable oil or shortening (for frying)
Combine ingredients, dry to wet, and drop batter by spoonfuls into hot oil (should be about 375 degrees). These doughnuts will turn themselves. When browned on each side, remove from oil, drain excess oil and roll in sugar. Simple & #Delish!

Ginger Nuts
½ cup whipping cream
¾ cup (4 ounces) crystallized ginger, finely chopped
1 tablespoon baking powder
1 tablespoon ground ginger
1 tablespoon vanilla extract
1 teaspoon salt
1¼ cups sugar
2 tablespoons (¼ stick) unsalted butter, melted, cooled
2 teaspoons grated lemon peel
3 large eggs
3½ cups all-purpose flour
GINGER TOPPING:
1½ cups sugar
2 teaspoons ground ginger
3 cups vegetable oil (for frying)
Whisk first 4 ingredients in a medium bowl to blend. Stir in crystallized ginger and lemon peel. Whisk sugar, eggs, and vanilla extract in a large bowl to blend well. Stir in cream and melted butter. Add dry ingredients and stir to blend well into a sticky dough. Cover bowl with plastic wrap; chill at least 1 hour. *For topping:* Mix sugar and ground ginger in medium bowl to blend. Line a large baking sheet with plastic wrap. Roll out dough on generously floured surface to ¾" thickness. Using floured 2¼" cookie cutter, cut out dough rounds. Using floured 1¼" cookie cutter, cut out hole in center of each large dough round, forming doughnuts. Gather dough scraps and reroll on floured surface. Repeat process, cutting out more doughnuts until all dough is used up. Place doughnuts on prepared baking sheet. Line another large baking sheet

with several layers of paper towels. Combine vegetable oil and shortening in a heavy large pot. Attach deep-fry thermometer inside pot. Heat oil mixture over medium heat until thermometer registers 350. Adjust heat as necessary to maintain temperature. Using slotted spoon, carefully lower 4 doughnuts into oil. Cook until bottoms turn a deep golden brown, about 2 minutes. Turn doughnuts over and cook about 2 minutes more. Using a slotted spoon, transfer doughnuts to paper-towel-lined baking sheet to drain. Cool slightly. While doughnuts are still warm, turn to coat in sugar topping. Repeat process with remaining doughnuts. Serve warm or at room temperature. #Delish!

Gingerbread Doughnuts
¼ cup cooking oil
¼ cup light molasses
½ cup packed brown sugar
½ cup sour cream
½ teaspoon baking soda
½ teaspoon salt
2 eggs
2 teaspoons ground ginger
2¾ cups flour
3 teaspoon baking powder
<u>LEMON GLAZE:</u>
2 cups sifted powdered sugar
2 tablespoons milk
1 teaspoon grated lemon peel
1 tablespoon lemon juice

Thoroughly stir together flour, baking powder, ginger, soda and salt. In a large mixer bowl, beat eggs until thick and lemon colored. Beat in sugar, sour cream, molasses, and the ¼ cup cooking oil. Stir in dry ingredients just until moistened. Roll out on lightly floured surface to 9" square about ¾" thick. Cut into nine strips 1" wide. Cut each strip in half crosswise. Shape strips of dough into 12" ropes. Fold in half; twist several times. Pinch ends to secure. Fry in deep hot oil (about 375 degrees) for about 2-3 minutes. Drain doughnuts on paper towels. *For glaze:* Combine and stir until smooth. Dip warm doughnuts in glaze. #Delish!

Golden Puffs
¼ cup granulated sugar
¼ cup vegetable oil
¾ cup milk
1 egg
1 tablespoon baking powder
1 teaspoon nutmeg or mace
1 teaspoon salt
2 cups sifted flour

Mix all dry ingredients together. Then add cooking oil, milk and egg. Mix thoroughly. Drop by small teaspoonful into deep, hot oil (about 375 degrees). Fry about 3 minutes or until golden brown. Drain on absorbent paper. Roll warm puffs in cinnamon-sugar or confectioners' sugar. Makes about three dozen. Simple & #Delish!

Holiday Eggnog Doughnuts

¼ cup butter or margarine
½ teaspoon salt
¾ teaspoon ground nutmeg
1 cup sour cream
1/3 cup granulated sugar
2 eggs
2 packages dry yeast
3-1/3 cups all-purpose flour, divided
Vegetable oil
<u>EGGNOG GLAZE:</u>
2 cups sifted confectioners' sugar
3 tablespoons commercial eggnog
Dash of ground nutmeg

Combine eggnog, butter, sugar and salt in a small saucepan; place over low heat and cook, stirring constantly, until butter melts. Set aside and let cool. Combine 2 cups flour, yeast and nutmeg; add warm eggnog mixture and mix well. Add eggs and beat at low speed with an electric mixer 30 seconds, scraping bowl constantly; beat at high speed an additional 3 minutes. Stir in remaining 1-1/3 cups flour, mixing well. Next, place dough in a greased bowl, turning to grease top. Cover and chill at least 2 to 3 hours. *To make glaze*: Combine all glaze ingredients and mix until smooth. Set aside. After about 3 hours, punch down the dough and turn out onto a lightly floured surface. Cover and let rest 10 minutes. Roll to 1/3" thickness, and cut with a floured doughnut cutter. Place doughnuts several inches apart on a greased baking sheet. Cover and let rise in a very warm place for about 45 to 50 minutes until very light. Heat 2" of oil in a large skillet to 375 degrees. Add doughnuts, a few at a time, and fry for 1½ to 2 minutes until golden brown on both sides, turning once. Drain well on paper towels. While still warm, dip top of each in the eggnog glaze. #Delish!

Honey-Maple Glazed Doughnuts

¼ cup oat flour
¼ pound butter
¼ teaspoon baking soda
¼ teaspoon lemon oil
¾ cup cooked and riced potato (2 to 3 potatoes, depending on size)
¾ cup light brown sugar, firmly packed
¾ teaspoon salt
1 cup milk, scalded
1 cup warm water
1 teaspoon baking powder
1 teaspoon sugar
1¼ teaspoon vanilla extract
1½ ounces fresh cake yeast
2 large eggs, plus 2 extra yolks
2-1/3 cups dry powdered milk
6 cups unbleached flour, plus additional as needed
3 pounds vegetable shortening, such as Crisco for a 4 quart fryer

HONEY MAPLE GLAZE:
¼ cup maple syrup
1 cup water
1 teaspoon honey
3 cups powdered sugar

Proof the yeast in 1 cup water with 1 teaspoon sugar. Add butter to the scalded milk. Then add the potato, brown sugar, eggs, egg yolks, vanilla, and lemon oil. Mix together the powdered milk, baking powder, soda, salt, oat flour, and unbleached flour. Add the proofed yeast mix to the other mix with milk, eggs, potato, etc. Add the flour mix to this. Knead, adding more flour if needed, to form a workable dough. Allow the dough to rise until doubled, about 45 minutes to 1 hour, then knead again. Roll out dough to a 1 to 1½" thickness and cut out rings using a doughnut cutter or a larger (3" to 4") and a smaller (2") biscuit cutter. Gather together the remaining dough and roll it again until all the dough is cut. Allow the cut doughnuts to rise again until doubled in size and then fry, making sure not to fry too many at a time. Fry in solid vegetable hot shortening (about 370 degrees) for about 30 to 45 seconds on each side. Glaze when slightly but not completely cool. Makes about 2½ dozen doughnuts. *To make glaze:* Combine all the glaze ingredients and either drizzle the glaze with a spoon over the slightly cooled doughnuts or dunk them into the glaze. Let glaze set about 10 minutes before serving. #Delish!

Huckleberry Fritters

¾ cup fresh huckleberries
¾ cup sugar
1 cup milk
1 egg, beaten
1 tablespoon baking powder
1½ cups all-purpose flour
Pinch of salt
Vegetable oil (for deep-frying)

Sift together dry ingredients; add berries. Mix egg and milk and add to dry mixture. Mix just until moistened Drop batter by tablespoonfuls into deep hot oil. Fry until golden brown, 3 to 4 minutes, turning once. Drain on paper towels. Sprinkle with powder sugar and serve warm. #Delish!

Italian Style Doughnuts

¼ teaspoon vanilla extract
½ cup confectioners' sugar for dusting
1 cup all-purpose flour
1 cup ricotta cheese
1 pinch salt
1½ teaspoons white sugar
2 eggs, beaten
2 quarts vegetable oil for frying
2 teaspoons baking powder

Heat oil in a deep-fryer to 375 degrees. In a medium heatproof bowl, combine the flour, baking powder, salt and sugar. Stir in the eggs, ricotta cheese and vanilla. Mix gently over low heat until combined. Batter will be sticky. Drop by tablespoons into the hot oil a few at a time. Doughnuts will turn over by themselves. Fry until golden brown, about 3 or 4 minutes. Drain excess oil and dust with confectioners' sugar. Serve warm. Makes three dozen. #Delish!

Juicy Jelly Doughnuts

¼ cup plus 2 tablespoons granulated sugar
¾ teaspoon salt
1 cup milk
1 egg, beaten
1 tablespoon lemon zest
1 tablespoon plus 1 teaspoon dry yeast
1 teaspoon cinnamon
1 teaspoon freshly grated nutmeg
2 cups raspberry filling
2 egg yolks
3 cups all-purpose flour
3 tablespoons melted butter
6 cups vegetable oil
Confectioners' sugar, for garnish
BERRY FILLING:
½ teaspoon cornstarch mixed with ½ teaspoon cold water
1 cup granulated sugar
1 pound raspberries plus ½ cup whole raspberries
1 tablespoon lemon juice

To prepare filling: In a saucepan, combine 1 pound raspberries, sugar and lemon juice. Cook over low heat until sugar dissolves and raspberries begin to break down. Remove from heat and transfer to a food processor. Puree until smooth. Strain through a fine mesh strainer into a saucepan. Cook over medium heat for 10 to 15 minutes, stirring occasionally. Add in ½ cup whole raspberries. Cook for 1 more minute. Remove from heat, whisk in cornstarch mixture. Return to high heat, bringing to a boil, whisking constantly until mixture is thick. Remove from the heat and cool. *To make doughnuts*: In a small saucepan, heat milk to a boil. Remove from heat, add sugar and cool Mix together warm milk and yeast and let sit for a few minutes. Transfer to a large bowl. Sift together flour, salt, cinnamon and nutmeg. Using a wooden spoon, add flour mixture to the milk mixture. Mix in egg yolks, melted butter and lemon zest. Turn mixture out onto a well-floured surface. Knead to form a dough. Place dough in a clean, lightly oiled bowl and cover with a towel. Place in a warm area and let rise for 1½ hours. After, remove dough from bowl and place on a floured surface. Roll out the dough to 1/8" thickness. Using a 3" round cookie cutter, cut the dough into 24 circles. Place 12 of the circles on a parchment lined sheet pan. Spoon 1 teaspoon of filling into the center of each circle. Brush beaten egg around the perimeter of each of the 12 circles. Place another circle on top of the raspberry filling and press around the edges to seal. Cover the tray with a towel and let rise another 30 minutes in a warm, draft-free location. In a large, deep pot, heat the oil to 325 degrees. When the doughnuts have risen, fry them in the oil, a few at a time, turning often until both sides are golden brown, about 6 minutes. Remove to a paper towel-lined plate and sprinkle with powdered sugar. #Delish!

Lemon Coconut Balls

¼ cup lemon juice
¼ cup melted butter
¼ cup sugar
½ cup flaked coconut
½ cup milk
½ teaspoon baking soda
1 egg
1 tablespoon baking powder
1 teaspoon salt
2 cups all-purpose flour
2 tablespoons grated lemon peel
Confectioner's sugar
Vegetable oil or shortening (for frying)

Combine flour, sugar, baking powder, salt, and baking soda in a mixing bowl. Combine milk, butter, lemon peel and juice, egg, and coconut in a separate bowl: beat well. Add liquid ingredients to dry ingredients Stir just until flour is moistened. Drop by teaspoonfuls into hot oil. Fry for 3 minutes or until golden brown. Drain on paper towels. Sprinkle with confectioners' sugar. #Delish!

Lemon Cream Cake Doughnuts

¼ cup sour cream
½ teaspoon baking soda
¾ cup granulated sugar
¾ cup plus 2 tablespoons nonfat buttermilk
1 tablespoon active dry yeast
1 tablespoon fresh lemon zest (omit if using vanilla extract)
1 teaspoon lemon or vanilla extract
1 teaspoon mace
1 teaspoon nutmeg
1 teaspoon salt
1¼ cup cake flour
1½ teaspoons baking powder
1-2 quarts canola oil
2½ cups all-purpose flour, divided
3 large eggs

Dust a large baking pan with ¼ cup flour. Place sour cream in small mixing bowl over hot water until sour cream is warm to the touch. Set aside. In large mixing bowl, combine 2 cups flour, cake flour, sugar, baking powder, baking soda, salt, nutmeg and mace. Make a well in center of dry ingredients. Place yeast in well. Pour warm sour cream over yeast and let sit 1 minute. While waiting, in a small mixing bowl, whisk together buttermilk, eggs, lemon extract and zest. Add to dry ingredients. By hand, using a wooden spoon or rubber spatula, gradually draw flour mixture into egg mixture and continue stirring until all flour is incorporated. *Note that the dough will be very sticky.* Sift 1/8 cup remaining flour onto clean work surface. Turn out dough. Sift another 1/8 cup flour over dough. Using your hands, pat the dough to an inch thickness. Using a doughnut cutter of your desired size (biscuit cutters work too), cut out the doughnuts, dipping cutter in flour before each cut. Let doughnuts rest 10 minutes. Next, heat oil in large deep fryer or stockpot to 375 degrees. Transfer 3 or 4 doughnuts at a time to hot oil and fry for 1½ minutes per side or until golden brown. Using a slotted spoon, transfer cooked doughnuts to a wire cooling rack. Repeat process until all doughnuts are cooked. Makes 1 dozen large doughnuts or 2 dozen smaller ones. #Delish!

Lingonberry Doughnuts
¼ cup (½ stick) unsalted butter
½ teaspoon salt
¾ cup whole milk
1 tablespoon dark rum
1 teaspoon grated lemon peel
2 cups all-purpose flour
3 large egg yolks
3 tablespoons sugar
5½ teaspoons dry yeast
Lingonberry or strawberry preserves
Powdered sugar
Vegetable oil (for deep-frying)
Heat milk and butter in heavy small saucepan over medium-high heat until butter melts, stirring occasionally. Transfer to large bowl. Cool for about 15 minutes. Whisk in yeast; let stand until yeast dissolves, about 8 minutes. Next, whisk yolks, rum, sugar, salt, and lemon peel into milk mixture. Stir in flour. Knead dough on floured surface 2 minutes. Lightly oil bowl. Add dough, turning to coat. Cover with plastic wrap, then towel. Let dough rise in warm draft-free area until doubled, about 1 hour. Punch down dough. Cover with plastic and towel; let rise 15 minutes. Divide dough in half. Divide each half into 10 equal pieces. Roll each piece between palm of hand and work surface to form smooth round ball. Place on baking sheet, spacing evenly. Cover with plastic wrap, then a towel. Let rise in warm area until almost doubled, about 15 minutes. Pour enough oil into medium pan to reach depth of 3". Heat to 325 degrees. Working in batches, fry doughnuts until brown, about 4 minutes per side. Using slotted spoon, transfer to paper towels and drain. Sift powdered sugar over doughnuts. Serve with preserves. Makes about 20 doughnuts. #Delish!

Mashed Potato Doughnuts
1 cup margarine
1 cup sugar
1½ teaspoon salt
2 cups mashed potatoes
2 packages yeast (mix according to package directions)
2 teaspoons nutmeg (optional)
4 cups scalded milk (cooled)
5 well beaten eggs
Flour
Vegetable oil or shortening (for frying)
Add soaked yeast to cooled milk, add sugar, eggs, margarine, salt, mashed potatoes, and nutmeg. Stir well; add enough flour to make soft dough. Let rise until double in

size, knead, and let rise again. Roll out to ½" thickness. Cut with doughnut cutter. Let rise for a ½ hour. Fry in hot oil. Remove when golden brown on each side and drain excess oil on paper towels. #Delish!

Mini-Maple Nuts
½ cup apple butter, or fruit puree fat replacement
½ teaspoon salt
1 large egg, lightly beaten
1/3 cup apple cider
1/3 cup maple syrup
1/3 cup nonfat plain yogurt
1½ teaspoons baking powder
1½ teaspoons baking soda
2 cups flour, all-purpose
2 teaspoons ground cinnamon
2/3 cup packed brown sugar
3 tablespoons canola oil
3 tablespoons granulated sugar, (approximately) for preparing pans
<u>VANILLA GLAZE:</u>
¼ cup maple syrup
1 teaspoon vanilla extract
1¼ cups confectioner's sugar

Preheat oven to 400 degrees. Thoroughly coat the molds of 2 mini-Bundt pans with nonstick cooking spray or oil. Sprinkle molds evenly with granulated sugar, tapping out the excess. (If you only have 1 pan, bake the recipe in 2 batches.) In a mixing bowl, whisk flour, baking powder, baking soda, salt and cinnamon; set aside. In another bowl, whisk egg, brown sugar, apple butter or fruit puree fat replacement, maple syrup, cider, yogurt and oil. Add the dry ingredients to the wet ingredients and stir just until moistened. Spoon about 2 generous tablespoons of batter into each prepared mold, smoothing the surface. Bake for 10 to 12 minutes, or until the tops spring back when touched lightly. Loosen edges and turn the doughnuts out onto a wire rack to cool. (If baking in 2 batches, cool the pan, clean it, and then recoat it with cooking spray or oil and sugar). *For Maple Glaze*: In a bowl, combine confectioners' sugar and vanilla. Gradually whisk in enough maple syrup to make a smooth, thick glaze. When the doughnuts are completely cool, set them, fluted-side up, in a wire rack over wax paper. Spoon some glaze over each doughnut, letting it drip down the sides. Makes 1 dozen doughnuts. #Delish!

Mouthwatering Molasses Doughnuts
¼ teaspoon ginger
¼ teaspoon sugar
¾ cup molasses
¾ teaspoon salt
1 cup milk or water
1 teaspoon baking powder
1 teaspoon baking soda
1 teaspoon cinnamon
1 teaspoon vanilla

2 eggs
2 tablespoons melted butter
4½ cups flour
Stir together 4½ cups of flour, baking soda, baking powder, cinnamon, salt and ginger; set aside. In large bowl blend molasses and sugar well with wooden spoon; beat in eggs and vanilla. Stir in flour mixture, milk/water and butter until smooth. Cover and chill for several hours. Turn out on a floured surface, work in more flour until not sticky. Roll out, cut with doughnut cutter. Fry in large fry pan, both sides, drain on paper towels. Roll in powdered sugar or sugar/cinnamon. #Delish!

New Orleans Style Doughnuts

¼ cup soft shortening
½ cup sugar
1 cup undiluted evaporated milk
1 package active dry yeast
1 teaspoon salt
1½ cups warm water
2 eggs
7 cups all-purpose flour
Oil for frying
Powdered sugar
In a large bowl, sprinkle yeast over water; stir to dissolve. Add sugar, salt, eggs and milk. Blend with beater until well blended. Add 4 cups of the flour; beat smooth. Add shortening; beat in remaining flour. Cover with plastic wrap and chill overnight. Roll out on floured board to 1/8" thickness. Cut into 2½" squares. Deep fry at 360 degrees for 2 to 3 minutes until lightly browned on each side. Drain on paper towels and sprinkle heavily with powdered sugar. #Delish!

Nutmeg Doughnuts

2 cups buttermilk
2 cups sugar
2 eggs
2 teaspoons baking soda
2 teaspoons ginger
2 teaspoons nutmeg
3 tablespoons butter
6 cups flour
Vegetable oil or shortening (for frying)
With a mixer, beat the eggs, sugar, and butter until light and fluffy. Add buttermilk and mix well. Sift and add flour, soda, nutmeg, and ginger. Roll out on a floured board and cut with a doughnut cutter. Fry in oil in iron skillet. Drain on paper towels. Roll in plain white sugar or a mixture of cinnamon and sugar while still warm. #Delish!

October Spice Doughnuts

¼ cup sugar
½ cup Egg Beaters
½ cup melted butter
1½ cups warm milk
1 cup cinnamon and sugar mix
1/3 cup vegetable shortening
1/3 cup warm water
2 packages dry yeast (about ½ ounces)
2 teaspoons nutmeg, fresh ground
2 teaspoons salt
4½ cups flour, all purpose

Sprinkle yeast over warm water and let dissolve for five minutes. Put milk and shortening in a small sauce pan and warm until shortening melts. Cool to lukewarm. Pour yeast mixture into a mixing bowl; add milk mixture and 2 cups flour. Beat briskly until well mixed. Add remaining flour and mix well. Cover the bowl and let rise in a warm place until doubled in size. Turn dough out onto floured surface. Dough will be soft, but still manageable. Pat it into a circle about ½" thick and cut doughnuts out with a 3" doughnut cutter. Place doughnuts on a greased baking sheet and let rise, uncovered for about 20 minutes and at 1" inch apart. Preheat oven to 450 degrees. Bake for 10 minutes or until lightly golden. Remove from oven and brush with melted butter. Sprinkle with cinnamon and sugar mix. Makes about 30 doughnuts. #Delish!

Old Fashioned Cake Doughnuts

¼ ground nutmeg
½ teaspoon salt
½ teaspoon vanilla
1 cup buttermilk
1 cup sugar
1 teaspoon baking soda
2 large eggs
2 tablespoons vegetable shortening
3½ cups all-purpose flour
4 teaspoons baking powder
Granulated sugar, powdered sugar or cinnamon and sugar
Vegetable oil or shortening (for frying)

In a medium bowl, whisk together the flour, baking powder, baking soda, salt and nutmeg. Set aside. In a large mixing bowl, using an electric mixer, cream the shortening and sugar together on medium speed until well blended. Add the eggs and vanilla and beat until well mixed. Stir in the flour mixture with buttermilk to the creamed mixture, stirring only until just mixed. Cover and refrigerate dough for at least 1 hour or overnight. Preheat oil in a deep fryer or Dutch oven to 375 degrees. On a lightly floured work surface, roll dough to about 3/8" thick. Cut out doughnuts using a floured cutter. Fry doughnuts until underside is golden brown, turn and brown the other side. Lift doughnuts out using a slotted spoon and drain on paper toweling. Put granulated sugar, powdered sugar, or cinnamon and sugar into a paper bag. Place warm doughnuts in bag and shake to coat well. Makes about three dozen doughnuts. #Delish!

Orange Glazed Doughnuts

¼ cup all-vegetable shortening
½ teaspoon salt
1 teaspoon grated orange peel
1 teaspoon vanilla
2 eggs, beaten
2 teaspoons baking powder
2/3 cup orange juice
2/3 cups granulated sugar
3¼ cups all-purpose flour
ORANGE GLAZE:
1 teaspoon grated orange peel
2 cups confectioners' sugar
3 tablespoons orange juice

Combine flour, baking powder and salt in small bowl. Combine eggs, granulated sugar and vanilla in large bowl. Beat at high speed of electric mixer until thick and lemon-colored. Combine peel, juice and ¼ cup melted Crisco. Add to egg mixture alternately with ¾ of flour mixture. Beat with electric mixer at medium-low speed just until blended after each addition. Stir in remaining flour mixture by hand. Cover. Chill for 2 hours. Heat about 3" Crisco to 365 degrees in deep fryer or deep saucepan. Flour rolling surface and pin lightly. Roll dough to 3/8" thickness. Cut with a floured 2½ inch doughnut cutter. Fry, a few at a time, in shortening heated to 365 degrees. Fry about 2 minutes or until golden brown. Turn once. Remove with slotted metal spoon. Drain on paper towels. *To make orange glaze*: Combine confectioners' sugar, one teaspoon grated orange peel and 3 tablespoons orange juice. Stir well and drizzle onto doughnuts. #Delish!

Oven-Baked Sour Cream Doughnuts

¼ cup granulated sugar
¼ teaspoon cinnamon
½ cup granulated sugar
½ cup sour cream
1 egg
1 teaspoon cinnamon
1 teaspoon ground nutmeg
2 cups Bisquick
3 tablespoons butter, melted

Heat oven to 425 degrees. Mix Bisquick, sugar, nutmeg, cinnamon, sour cream and egg until soft dough forms. Gently smooth dough into a ball on a floured cloth-covered board. Knead 10 times. Roll dough to ½" thickness. Cut with a floured 2½" doughnut cutter. Lift doughnuts carefully with a spatula and place about 2" apart on an ungreased cookie sheet. Bake until golden brown, 8 to 10 minutes. Next, mix ½ cup sugar and 1 teaspoon cinnamon. Immediately brush entire doughnut with melted butter; dip into sugar mixture, coating all sides. Or, if desired, spread with a confectioners' sugar. Makes 10 to 12 #delish doughnuts.

Potluck Cake Doughnuts

¼ ground nutmeg
½ teaspoon salt
½ teaspoon vanilla
1 cup buttermilk
1 cup sugar
1 teaspoon baking soda
2 large eggs
2 tablespoons vegetable shortening
3½ cups all-purpose flour
4 teaspoon baking powder
Vegetable oil or shortening (for frying)

Granulated sugar, powdered sugar or cinnamon and sugar for garnish. In a medium bowl, whisk together the flour, baking powder, baking soda, salt and nutmeg. Set aside. In a large mixing bowl, using an electric mixer, cream the shortening and sugar together on medium speed until well blended; add the eggs and vanilla and beat until well mixed. Alternately stir in the flour mixture with buttermilk to the creamed mixture, stirring only until just mixed. Cover and refrigerate dough for at least 1 hour or overnight. Preheat oil in a deep fryer or Dutch oven heated to 375 degrees. On a lightly floured work surface, roll dough to about 3/8" thick. Cut out doughnuts using a floured cutter. Fry doughnuts until underside is golden brown, turn and brown the other side. Lift doughnuts out using a slotted spoon and drain on paper toweling. Put granulated sugar, powdered sugar, or cinnamon and sugar into a paper bag. Place warm doughnuts in bag and shake to coat well. This recipe makes a large batch of about 36. #Delish!

Powdered Doughnuts I

½ cup granulated sugar
1 cake yeast
1 teaspoon salt
3 cups milk
3 tablespoons unsalted butter
5 egg yolks
6 cups flour
Vegetable oil or shortening (for frying)

Mix yeast & sugar in lukewarm water; let stand. Mix together egg yolks, butter and yeast mixture. Add flour and make a soft dough. Mix well with a wooden spoon; let stand 1 hour. *Do not knead.* Place doughnut dough on a floured board, and pat out to about a 1" thickness with your hands and not rolling pans. Cut out doughnuts and allow them to stand for 45 minutes. Deep fry in hot oil until golden brown. Remove, drain and sprinkle with powdered sugar. #Delish!

Powdered Sugar Doughnuts II

½ teaspoon salt
1 cup sweet milk
1 teaspoon baking soda
1½ cups sugar
2 teaspoons cream of tartar
3 eggs
3 tablespoons butter; melted
Dash nutmeg
Flour
Grated lemon peel
Vegetable oil or shortening (for frying)

Beat eggs well and add sugar. Mix well. Add milk, salt, butter, cream of tartar and baking soda. Beat well. Next, add nutmeg and lemon. Add enough flour to make a soft dough. Roll out about ½" thick and cut with a double cutter or two different size biscuit cutters. Let doughnuts dry for about 10 minutes before frying in hot oil. Roll in powdered sugar. Makes about 3 dozen #delish doughnuts.

Pretty Peach Fritters

½ cup sugar
½ teaspoon lemon juice
½ teaspoon salt
½ teaspoon vanilla
1 cup milk
1/3 cup butter
1½ cups chopped peaches (fresh or canned)
2 cups flour
2 eggs, well beaten
3 teaspoons baking powder
Vegetable oil (for deep-frying)

Cream the butter and sugar. Add the eggs and beat thoroughly. Sift the dry ingredients together and add alternately with the milk. Fold in the peaches, lemon juice and vanilla. Drop by teaspoonfuls into hot Crisco or lard (heated to about 375 degrees) and fry until golden brown. Drain excess oil and let cool just slightly. #Delish!

Pumpkin Doughnuts

¼ teaspoon ground ginger
½ cup buttermilk
½ teaspoon baking soda
½ teaspoon cinnamon
1 cup fresh pumpkin puree or canned pumpkin
1 cup sugar
1 teaspoon nutmeg
2 eggs, beaten
2 tablespoons oil
2 teaspoons salt
4 cups flour

4 teaspoons baking powder
Powdered sugar, for coating
Shortening for frying

In a large bowl, beat eggs and sugar until light and fluffy. Add oil, pumpkin and buttermilk. Mix well. Next, combine dry ingredients and add to egg mixture. Chill for 1 hour. Turn out on floured board and roll to a ½" thickness. Use a doughnut cutter to cut out doughnuts. Deep fry (hot grease...about 375 degrees) until brown on one side. Flip and brown other side. Drain well on paper towels and roll in sugar. #Delish!

Purely Pineapple Doughnuts
¼ teaspoon nutmeg
1 (8½ ounce) can crushed pineapple
1 egg, slightly beaten
2 cups biscuit mix
3 tablespoons granulated sugar
Vegetable oil (for deep-frying)
<u>PINEAPPLE GLAZE:</u>
1 cup sifted confectioners' sugar
1½ tablespoons pineapple syrup (reserve 1½ tablespoons for glaze)

To pineapple, add egg, biscuit mix, sugar and nutmeg; stir into stiff dough. Heat oil to 375 degrees. Drop dough by teaspoonful into hot oil; fry to golden brown, about 3 minutes, turning once. Remove with slotted spoon; drain on paper towels. Dip some of the doughnuts into pineapple glaze, others in confectioners' sugar. Serve warm. #Delish!

Raspberry Jam Doughnuts
½ cup sugar, for dusting
½ teaspoon salt
¾ teaspoon ground cinnamon
1 (12 ounce) jar seedless raspberry jam
1 large egg, lightly beaten
1 tablespoon light corn oil, plus more for bowl
1 teaspoon active dry yeast
1/3 cup milk
2 cups all-purpose flour, plus more for dusting
2 tablespoons honey
2 tablespoons warm water
3 cups peanut oil

In a medium bowl, combine yeast with warm water, and let stand until foamy, about 5 minutes. Whisk in honey, ¼ teaspoon cinnamon, egg, milk, and corn oil. Using a wooden spoon, stir in salt and flour. Mix until dough appears smooth. Transfer dough to a lightly oiled bowl, cover tightly with plastic wrap and set in a warm place to rise until doubled in size. This will take about 1½ hours. Next, line a baking sheet with parchment and another with paper towels; set aside. Turn out dough onto a lightly floured work surface, and knead four to five times. Roll dough into a 10" square, about ¼" thick. Using a pizza cutter, cut into 2.5" x 2.5" squares, and transfer to parchment-lined baking sheet. Lightly cover with plastic; let rest in a warm place 20 minutes. In a medium saucepan, heat peanut oil until a deep fryer thermometer registers 360 degrees. Working in batches of five or six, fry doughnuts until golden brown on both sides. Using a slotted spoon, transfer to the paper-towel-lined baking sheet to drain. Fry remaining doughnuts. In a medium bowl, combine sugar and the remaining ½ teaspoon cinnamon. Toss the doughnuts lightly in cinnamon sugar. Fill a pastry bag fitted with a #4 tip with raspberry jam. Using a wooden skewer or toothpick, make a tiny hole in the side of each doughnut. Fit the pastry tip into a hole and pipe about 1 tablespoon of jam into the doughnut. Repeat with remaining doughnuts. Toss filled doughnuts in cinnamon sugar again to fully dust, if desired. Serve immediately. #Delish!

Sour Cream & Banana Doughnuts

¼ teaspoon nutmeg
½ cup honey
½ cup sour cream
½ teaspoon baking soda
½ teaspoon salt
½ teaspoon vanilla
1 banana
2 eggs
2 tablespoons butter or margarine
2½ cups flour
2½ teaspoons baking powder
Vegetable oil or shortening (for frying)

Sift together dry ingredients. Beat eggs until light. Add honey gradually and continue beating until well mixed. Beat in mashed banana, butter, sour cream and vanilla. Stir in flour mixture to make a soft dough. Chill 2 hours or longer. Roll out on floured board about ¼" thick. Cut with doughnut cutter. In deep fat heated to 370 degrees, fry a few at a time and then move on to the doughnut holes. Turn doughnuts when they rise to the surface and are brown on the underside. Fry until brown on both sides. Remove from fat and drain thoroughly. #Delish!

Sourdough Applesauce Doughnuts

¼ cup buttermilk
½ cup applesauce
½ cup sourdough starter
½ cup sugar
½ teaspoon baking soda
½ teaspoon cinnamon
½ teaspoon nutmeg
½ teaspoon vanilla
1 teaspoon salt
1½ teaspoon baking powder
2 egg yolks
2 tablespoons shortening
2-2/3 cups flour

Knead all ingredients well. Roll out and cut into doughnuts. Let stand for a while. Heat shortening to 390 degrees. Fry doughnuts, drain and dust or frost as desired. #Delish!

Southern Sweet Milk Doughnuts
1 cup milk
1 cup sugar
1 tablespoon butter
1 teaspoon nutmeg
1 teaspoon salt
2 eggs
3 teaspoons baking powder
Flour
Vegetable oil or shortening (for frying)
Beat the eggs till very light, add the sugar and when foamy add melted butter. Sift the baking powder, salt and nutmeg with one cup of flour and stir into first mixture, alternating with the milk so as to keep the mixture smooth. Add just enough flour to make a soft dough which can be handled. Roll out to ¾" on a lightly floured board. A soft dough makes light, tender doughnuts when cooked. Fry in deep fat and drain on paper towels. Roll the doughnuts in powdered sugar just before serving. #Delish!

Spiced Maple Doughnuts
¼ cup butter or margarine, melted
¼ teaspoon ground cinnamon
¼ teaspoon ground ginger
½ cup granulated sugar
½ cup maple-flavored syrup
½ teaspoon baking soda
½ teaspoon ground nutmeg
1 teaspoon salt
1/3 cup buttermilk or sour milk
2 eggs
2 teaspoons baking powder
3 cups all-purpose flour
Shortening or cooking oil for frying
Sifted powdered sugar
In a mixing bowl stir together flour, baking powder, salt, baking soda, nutmeg, cinnamon, and ginger; set aside. In large mixer bowl, beat together eggs, granulated sugar and maple-flavored syrup till thick. Stir in buttermilk and melted butter. Add flour mixture to egg mixture, stirring until just blended. Cover; chill dough about 2 hours. When ready, turn dough out onto lightly floured surface. Roll to ½" thickness. Cut with floured 2½" doughnut cutter. Fry, a few at a time, in deep, hot fat (about 375 degrees) for 1 minute per side or till golden brown, turning once. Drain on paper towels. Cool. Dust with powdered sugar. Makes 18 to 20 doughnuts. #Delish!

Strawberry Fields Doughnuts

1 packet refrigerated fresh dough for buttermilk biscuits
Confectioner's sugar
Oil for deep-frying
Ripe strawberries, rinsed, drained, hulled
Sugar or confectioner's sugar

Heat oil for deep frying to 365 degrees. Meanwhile, separate biscuit dough into biscuits, cut each in half, and flatten into rounds about 1/8" thick. Place a ripe strawberry (coated with sugar or confectioner's sugar) in the center of each round of dough. Gather edge to the top and twist or pinch to seal. Fry doughnuts, a few at a time, in heated oil about 2 minutes, or until browned, turning occasionally. Drain. Sift confectioner's sugar generously over hot doughnuts and serve immediately. Interior will be extremely juicy and hot...#Delish!

Sugar Cane Doughnuts

½ stick unsalted butter, melted
½ teaspoon baking soda
¾ cup well-shaken buttermilk
1½ teaspoons salt
12 cups vegetable oil
2 large eggs
2 teaspoons baking powder
2¼ cups sugar
3½ cups all-purpose flour

Sift together flour, baking powder, salt, and baking soda in a large bowl. Whisk together 1 cup sugar, buttermilk, butter, and eggs in another bowl, then add to flour and stir until a dough forms (dough will be sticky). Turn out dough onto a well-floured surface and knead gently 8 times. Flour dough and a rolling pin, then roll out dough into a 12" round (about 1/3" thick). Cut out as many doughnuts as possible with a floured 3" doughnut cutter and transfer to lightly floured baking sheets. Gather scraps, reroll, and cut more doughnuts in same manner. Heat oil in a 5-quart heavy pot until thermometer registers 375 degrees. Working in batches of 3, slide doughnuts into oil and fry. Once each doughnut floats to surface, turn over and fry for 50 seconds. Turn again and fry 50 additional seconds. Transfer to paper towels to drain. Cool slightly and dredge in remaining 1¼ cups sugar. Makes about 18 doughnuts. #Delish!

Sugar N' Spice Doughnuts

¼ teaspoon cinnamon
½ teaspoon ground cloves
¾ teaspoon nutmeg
1 cup milk
1 cup sugar
1 teaspoon salt
2 eggs, beaten
3 tablespoons shortening
4 cups flour
4 teaspoons baking powder

SPICED ICING:
¾ cup sugar
1/8 teaspoon ground cloves
1/8 teaspoon nutmeg
2 teaspoons cinnamon
Cream shortening. Add sugar and eggs. Sift flour, spices, baking powder, and salt together and add alternately with milk to the first mixture. The dough should be fairly soft. Roll out to about ½"thick onto a floured surface. Cut with doughnut cutter. Fry in deep fat at 375 degrees until brown, turning once (about 1½ minutes on each side). Drain excess oil. Makes 2 dozen doughnuts. *For icing:* Roll doughnuts in coating (or shake in a bag). #Delish!

Summer Squash Doughnuts

½ teaspoon cinnamon
½ teaspoon nutmeg
½ teaspoon salt
1 cup cooked squash
1 cup milk
1 teaspoon vanilla
1¼ cup sugar
2 eggs, well beaten
2 tablespoons shortening
3 cups flour
3 teaspoons baking powder
Cream shortening and sugar. Add eggs, squash and flavoring. Sift flour, measure and sift with salt, baking powder and spices. Add alternately with milk to first mixture. Chill dough. Turn onto a lightly-floured board. Roll in sheet 1/3" thick. Cut with floured cutter. Fry in deep fat (365 degrees) until brown. Drain and serve warm.

Sunday Dinner Doughnuts

½ cup sugar
1 to 2 tablespoons grated orange rind
2 eggs
2 teaspoons vanilla
2/3 cup milk
4 cups Bisquick
Vegetable oil
CHOCOLATE ICING:
¼ cup boiling water
2 squares unsweetened chocolate (2 ounces)
2 tablespoons butter
3 cups sifted powdered sugar
Heat deep fat to 375 degrees. Mix all ingredients, beat vigorously 25 to 30 strokes. Turn dough onto a floured surface, knead 10 times. Roll out 3/8" thick. Cut with a floured doughnut cutter and place in hot fat. Fry 1 to 2 minutes per side. Remove and drain on absorbent paper. *To make icing*: Melt 2 unsweetened chocolate and butter. Remove from heat and blend in 3 cups sifted powdered sugar and ¼ cup boiling water. Beat until smooth and glaze doughnuts. #Delish!

Sweet Treat Doughnut Holes

½ teaspoon vanilla extract
1 cup confectioners' sugar
1 tablespoon margarine
1 to 2 tablespoons milk
2 tablespoons melted margarine
7½ ounces refrigerated buttermilk biscuits
SUGAR COATING:
1 ½ teaspoons cinnamon
2 tablespoons granulated sugar

Preheat oven to 450 degrees. Line a baking sheet with parchment paper or coat with nonstick spray, set aside. Open the can of biscuits and separate them into 10 biscuits. Cut each biscuit into 4 equal pieces. Roll each piece into a ball. Dip the balls in the melted margarine. Roll the entire ball until well coated. Place on a baking sheet about ½" apart. Bake for 6 to 7 minutes or until just beginning to brown. Remove from oven and cool. In a small bowl, mix together the confectioners' sugar, margarine, vanilla and milk. Blending until smooth. Combine the sugar and cinnamon in a small bowl, set aside. Dip each cooled doughnut into the glaze. Roll some in the sugar/cinnamon mixture and leave others with glaze. #Delish!

Sweet Cream Doughnuts

½ teaspoon salt
¾ cup sugar
1 cup sweet cream
1 cup vegetable oil
10 cups flour
2 packages yeast soaked in ½ cup water
5 cups boiling water
5 egg yolks

Pour boiling water over oil, sugar, cream and salt. Cool to lukewarm. Add yeast and egg yolks, well beaten. Add flour and knead well. Let rise about 2 hours. Roll and cut out. Then let rise for ½ hour and fry in deep fat until golden brown. Drain and dust with powdered sugar or frost one side with vanilla frosting. #Delish!

Traditional Raised Doughnuts

¼ cup water, lukewarm
¾ cup sugar, granulated
1 cup milk, scald & cool
1 egg, well beaten
1 package dry yeast
1 tablespoon sugar, granulated
1 teaspoon salt
1½ cups flour, sifted
1½ teaspoons nutmeg
3 cups flour sifted
3 tablespoons butter or margarine
Melted shortening

Powdered sugar for dusting
Vegetable oil or shortening (for frying)

Scald Milk. Cool to lukewarm in a large bowl. Sprinkle yeast in lukewarm water. Let stand for 5-10 min., until dissolved. Stir up; stir into milk with 1 tablespoon sugar. Add 1½ cups flour; beat well with hand or electric beater. Cover with a clean towel; to let rise in warm place for about 1 hour. Work butter with a spoon until creamy. Add ¾ cup sugar gradually, while beating with the spoon until light. Add egg, nutmeg and salt; stir into yeast mixture. Add 3 cups flour; place in a well-greased bowl. Brush dough with melted fat; cover with clean towel; let rise until double in bulk. Turn out on a floured board, roll ½" thick. Cut with floured doughnut cutter. Place on a floured board and cover, and let each rise in warm place until double in size. Next, fry doughnuts in 1½" grease heated to 375 degrees. As soon as doughnuts rise to surface, turn to brown the other side. Remove and drain excess fat. Cool and dust with powdered sugar, or a cinnamon and sugar mixture. Can also be frosted if desired. #Delish!

Very Vanilla Doughnuts

¼ teaspoon nutmeg
¾ cup milk
1 cup sugar
1 teaspoon salt
1 teaspoon soft shortening
1 teaspoon vanilla
2 eggs
2 teaspoons baking powder
2¼ cups flour

Sift dry ingredients together in a large bowl and add shortening. Beat eggs, vanilla, milk and mix for ½ minute. Drop in hot grease, turning once. Drain on paper towels. Cool. Frost one side with white vanilla frosting (and sprinkles if desired). #Delish!

White Chocolate Cake Doughnuts

¼ teaspoon salt
½ cup milk
1 cup chocolate glaze
1 cup chopped macadamia nuts
1 teaspoon vanilla
2 beaten eggs
2 ounces melted white chocolate
2 tablespoons melted butter
2 teaspoons baking powder
2/3 cup sugar
3¼ cup flour
Vegetable oil or shortening (for frying)

Preheat the fryer. In a mixing bowl, sift the flour, baking powder and salt together. In a mixing bowl, whisk the eggs and sugar together. Add the melted chocolate and butter. Stir in the milk and vanilla. Slowly add the sifted flour into the egg mixture, incorporate into a soft dough. Cover the dough and chill for 2 hours. Turn the dough out onto a floured surface. Roll the dough out to ½" thick. Cut the doughnuts out, using a 2½" doughnut cutter. Fry a couple of doughnuts at a time for 1 minute on each side. Remove the doughnuts from the fryer and drain excess grease. Place the doughnuts on a wire rack. Drizzle the warm doughnuts with the chocolate glaze and sprinkle with the macadamia nuts. Place the doughnuts on a platter. Makes 1 dozen doughnuts. #Delish!

World's Easiest Doughnuts
½ teaspoon salt
1 cup buttermilk
1 cup white sugar
1 teaspoon soda
2 teaspoons baking powder
2 teaspoons cinnamon
2 teaspoons nutmeg
3 tablespoons cider vinegar
3 tablespoons Crisco
4 cups cake flour
4 eggs
Combine sugar, eggs, Crisco in electric mixer. Beat on high speed for 2 minutes. Add buttermilk, vinegar, salt. Beat at slow speed for ½ minute. Sift flour, soda, baking powder and spices together. Fold in, but do not beat. Allow to sit in the refrigerator overnight. The next day, use a doughnut cutter to cut treats to your preferred size. Fry in oil or Crisco, a few at time, at about 375 degrees. Drain excess oil and serve warm. Dust with cinnamon and sugar if desired. #Delish!

Yummy Buttermilk Doughnuts
¼ cup unsalted butter, melted
½ teaspoon ground ginger
½ teaspoon salt
1 cup granulated sugar
1 teaspoon baking soda
1 teaspoon ground cinnamon
1½ teaspoons vanilla extract
2 large eggs
2 teaspoons baking powder
2/3 cup buttermilk
3¼ cups all-purpose flour
Confectioners' or cinnamon sugar for coating
Vegetable oil for deep frying
In a large bowl, sift together ginger, salt, soda, cinnamon, baking powder and flour. In another large bowl, using hand-held electric mixer set at medium high speed, beat eggs, granulated sugar until combined. In a small bowl, stir together buttermilk, butter and vanilla until combined. Beat this mixture into egg mixture. With mixer set on low speed, add flour mixture; beat just until smooth. Cover dough; refrigerate about 1 hour. In a fryer or stockpot, heat oil to 375 degrees. While oil is heating, cut out doughnuts. On well-floured surface, with floured rolling pin or floured hands, roll or pat dough out to ½" thick. With a floured doughnut cutter, cut out doughnuts and holes. Gather scraps together; reroll, cutting out doughnuts and holes until all dough

is used. Fry doughnuts, three or so at a time, for 30 to 60 seconds on each side or until golden, turning once with slotted spoon. Lift from hot oil with slotted spoon; drain on layers of paper towels or wire rack. Repeat with remaining doughnuts and holes, cooking about eight holes at a time. Serve as is, or shake in bag with granulated, confectioners or cinnamon sugar. Makes about 16 doughnuts, or twice as many holes. #Delish!

Thank you for your purchase!
May you enjoy and be well!

ABOUT THE AUTHOR

I am a Tennessee native and a connoisseur of good eats. My culinary delights are inspired by my Southern roots.

I am from cornbread and cabbage, fried chicken and Kool-Aid soaked lemon slices.

I am from hen houses, persimmon trees and juicy, red tomatoes on the vine.

I am from sunflowers growing wild in summer and homemade ice cream in the winter.

I am from family reunions, blue collar men, happy housewives, and Sunday dinners.

I am from spiritual folks who didn't always get it right, but believed in the power of prayer – and taught it to their kids.

I am from the hottest of hot summers and kids running barefoot and free through thirsty Tennessee grass.

I am from a grandmother who sang gospel that was magic...song drenched air would tumble from her lungs, leap into your spirit and make you feel fantastic things.

I am from hard, heartfelt lessons about living and kitchens full of the perfume of love.

♥♥♥ *This book is from my heart to yours.* ♥♥♥

For info, freebies & new book notices, follow @SoDelishDish on social media!
Scan with your smartphone!

FIND MORE BOOKS ONLINE

Printed in Poland
by Amazon Fulfillment
Poland Sp. z o.o., Wrocław